CW00536170

SHOREDITCH WILD LIFE

SHOREDITCH WILD LIFE

by Dougie Wallace

HOXTON MINI PRESS

Book One

I've Lived in East London for 86½ Years

Book Two

East London Swimmers

Book Three

A Portrait of Hackney

Book Four

Shoreditch Wild Life

Book Five

One Day Young in Hackney

Book Six

Drivers in the 1980s

Book Seven

Columbia Road

Book Eight

Lost in the City

Book Nine

Hackney by Night

East London Photo Stories

Book Four

SHOREDITCH:
THE RICHNESS AND WRONGNESS OF IT ALL

Messy, absurd, hilarious, and full to the brim with the joy of being alive on a sunny weekend in Shoreditch, these pictures fizz with the throbbing life-force of this peculiar square mile of East London. Big black blokes dressed head to pointy toe in gold lamé, a girl squatting in cowboy boots with a plastic pint glass who has the look of someone who's not quite sure what party she's at anymore, wasted women who look like the best kind of trouble, and all the while there's a crashed car upside down in the street while the party gets madder all around it: in short, total fucking chaos, a chaos I've never seen so condensed into one square mile anywhere else. I didn't know people lived like this before I moved to Shoreditch as a young man, and now, all these years later, as somebody who's much more likely to be walking his dog round the park than stuck five hours into a drinking session come Saturday evening, I still can't quite believe they do.

As much as he captures the mad night out, Dougie also gets the morning after - specifically, the equally off-kilter, spontaneous street theatre of Brick Lane market. Is the girl striking a pose for a fashion shoot or just for the passers by? What, really, is the difference anyhow? These streets are one big fashion parade. They feel like a slightly demented parallel reality, a pocket of weirdness and colour, the Ditch beyond the Roman wall of the City where all the tat and flotsam Shore up, the no-man's-land where everything mad and messy collides: *roll up, roll up, come and get your plastic pink flamingoes, two for the price of one!* There's lots of pink in these photos, and lots of gold lamé: glamour on the cheap, creating glamour out of nothing, which says a lot about the spirit of Shoreditch.

Dougie's work is often about mismatches and juxtapositions: the head-on collision of the trendies and the old East End market traders, a car crash of different sensibilities that don't belong together, an old bloke selling stuff off his stall with a motorbike helmet on, surrounded by stolen bikes and trendy graffiti, pensioners with walking sticks in 90s rave clothes, horrified old Bangladeshi ladies bemused by the rake-thin young chap at a bus stop wearing the bindi and little Indian dress.

Ultimately, I think, *Shoreditch Wild Life* is about the adventure of getting lost in cities: the strangeness of looking at the streets, the kaleidoscope bloom of the flower market, a sensory overload, a world far too complex and full of difference to possibly understand, especially if you're a bit all over the shop come Sunday morning. For a moment it seems as if a poster of a lady in a pimped-up sports car miraculously comes to life, and she steps out onto streets strewn with cigarette multi-packs and cardboard boxes. Fantasy merges with reality, just as it probably did for Dougie one bleary-eyed Sunday morning, all the wrong connections joining up into wonderful, impossible scenes, at least for the brief split-second of a photograph.

Michael Smith
East London, 2014

CANAL

EMPRESS
COACHES
EST 1923
739 5454

TO LONDON

STOWAWAYS SC
TROJAN RECORDS
SKA
WALTHAMSTOW
STOWAWAYS

BRICK

SONY

TELEPHONE

BLITZ BLITZ
VINTAGE CLOTHING 40S-90S ACCESSORIES
HOMEWARE VINTAGE FURNITURE JEWELLERY
WATCHES SUNGLASSES POSTERS BOOKS LUGGAGE
COFFEE SHOP VINTAGE BIKES RECLAIMED ECCENTRICITIES
BLITZ
CASIO
WATER RESIST

Open House London

Evening Standard

COCAINE
FOUND IN
WRAP OF
LONDON
COCAINE

Evening
Standrd

The Dove
BRUNCH

POLICE

WARNING
CCTV

24 HOUR
CAR.PAR
RALEIGH

24 HOUR
ARPARK
24 HOUR
CARPARK

YARD SALE
OPEN

LUPINS
EVERY YEAR
4 pots
£8

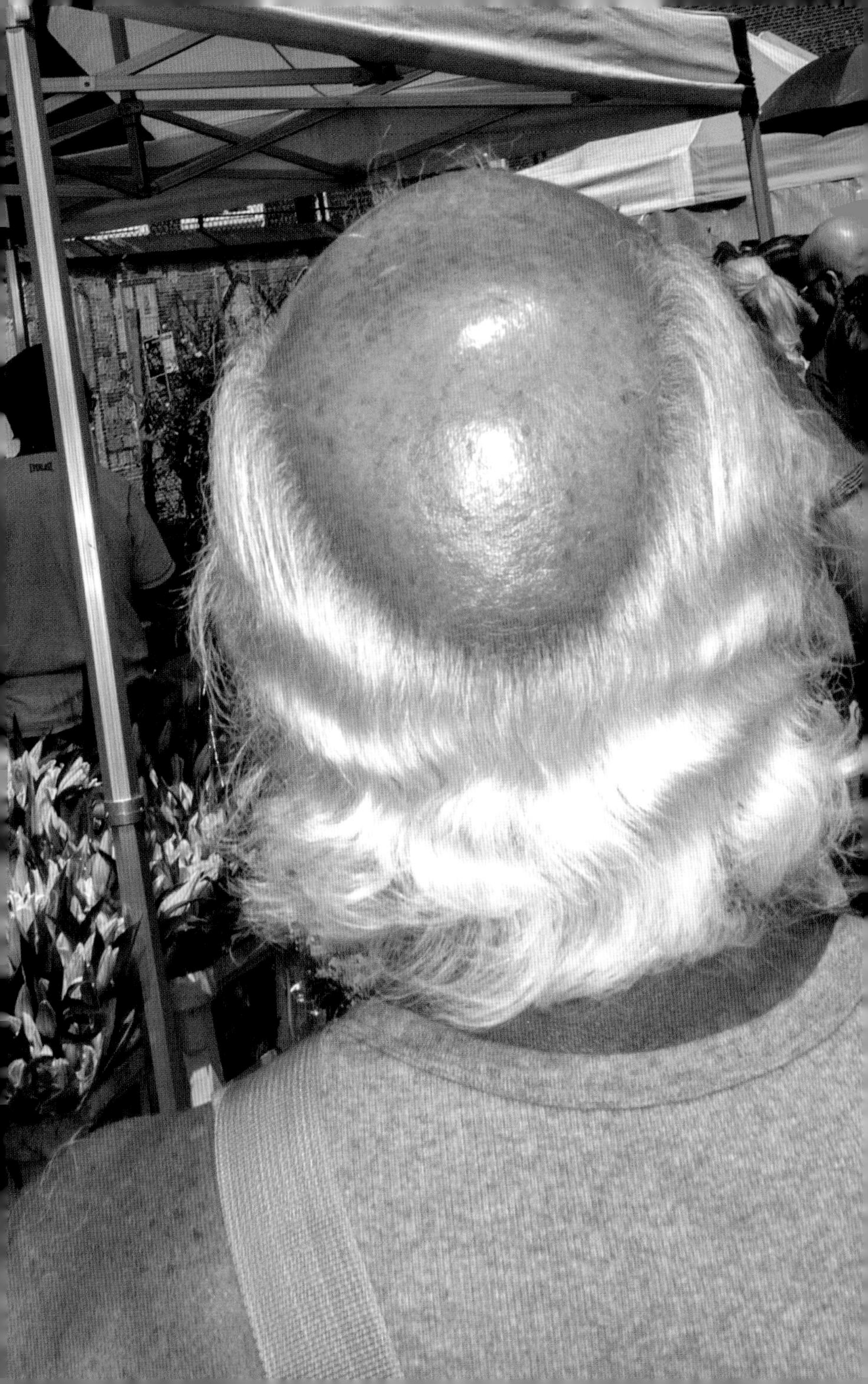

ABRUPT
EROTICA
smut while
U wait!
phone
whore

Come In
OPEN
25%
EXTRA!

agv

UESDAYS
STREET
ART TOURS
ART
IS
TOWER HAMLETS
ENFORCEMENT OFFICER
MARKETS
5
5
Palette
wellman
tricologic
man
hair growth
Grecian

JUST FOR MEN
JUST FOR MEN
JUST FOR MEN
JUST FOR MEN
£5.
£5.
JUST FOR

LONSDALE
LONDON

OAK

TRUMAN
HANBURY
BUXTON
let by

FISH

MOTHER CLUCKER
NEW YORK STYLE
BEEF BRISKET
THE HOME OF
MEAT PORN
CHEESE BURGERS
Pulled Pork
Beef Brisket
#Meat Porn

DEENEY'S
Scottish Flavour
TOASTIES
MACBETH
MACBETH
MACBETH
CHEESE
DEENEY'S
Scottish Flavour

Marsha Shanks
6920 Yarborough Ln.
Lakeland FL 33812

GERIA

East London
CSV

www.met.police.uk

VINTAG
DEPT.
STOR

WHITECHAPEL ART GALLERY

POLICE
JCJ

Night buses in east

End of
bus lane

KUR PAZA
LAMA

14/18/22ct
GOLD

Street 8
SHOREDITCH
17239
London
X239 NND

LEVI'S
VINTAGE CLOTHING

WHITE CUBE
CRU

THE MOTELS

GIRLS

THOMPSON'S
P591 WRU

FOPS

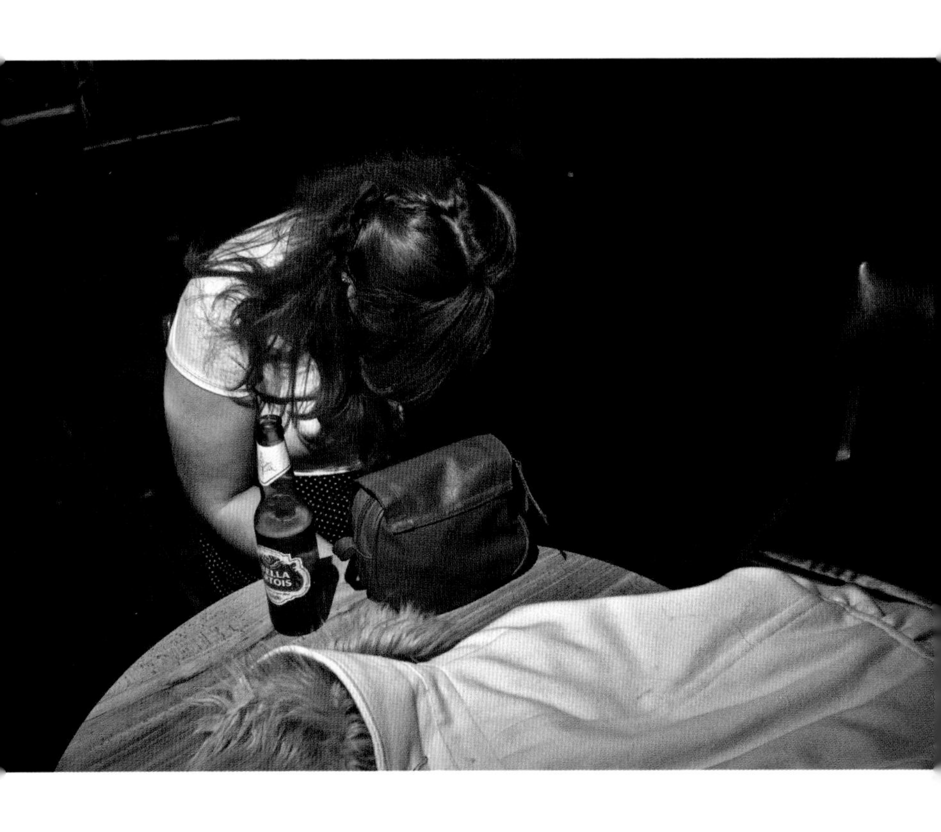
ELLA
TOIS